To Emme

Enjoy the history
& the story.
Keep writing!

Nzade Zimele Keita
2/94

BIRTHMARKS

Ben McMichael III

nzadi zimele keita

NIGHTSHADE PRESS
©Copyright 1993 by Nzadi Zimele Keita

ISBN 1-879205-39-4
Editor: Carolyn Page
Book Design: Roy Zarucchi
Cover Collage: Carolyn Page
Artwork: Carolyn Page & Ben McMichael III
Disk Preparation: Anne-Marie Miller

Acknowledgments

Some of the poems in this collection have appeared in *Potato Eyes* and *Shooting Star Review*.

Reverent thanks to my "voices" for their rivers of memory: Anna Hook Bantom, Mabel Elizabeth Harrison, Emmett Bailey, Lillian Johnson, Anna Mae Ellison Chaney, James Chaney Sr., Rev. Henry H. Nichols, and Rev. Marguerite Miles.

Gratitude also to those who have supported this work with any word, wish or effort; most specifically to Ramona Hyman and Sonia Sanchez. Also Huey Cotton, Miyoshi Smith, Jane Todd Cooper, Lamont Steptoe, Aaren Perry, Sandra Gould Ford, E. Ethelbert Miller and Reggie Young.

NIGHTSHADE PRESS
PO Box 76
Troy, Maine 04987
(207)948-3427

First Edition
Printed in USA

To my elders,
my family,
my husband,
and especially,
to Najja and Cabral

CONTENTS

MAYDEE STREET

fresh cream and dinner pails
tall, pecan-filled grasses

long reaches
of air and sun and rain;

the fields, the water pump
and the race between;

the animals, flinching and
singing to a melted sky.

SUNDAY

floral
ladies fanning
on the downbeat, bring Him
sopranos trained over
mops and
linens

JEKYLL ISLAND

The women wore rice and figs
and fishes into town,
stored in a basket of braids

The men entered the morning
before its birth
in sharp boats cut like melons

Some seasons, the water imitated
their tongue, a language
spilling incantations

Old folks say
they laid down cowrie shells
with the crops
an' when the shells dried up,
floods came, swarmin' the moss
an' weevils came, troublin' the harvest
an' the pearl waters opened
to the big yachts,
like circlin' vultures,
bringin'
white linen smiles on black butlers,
New York buyers
and country clubs, set down on the spirit-place

Old folks say the land closed
over their bones
and bones populated
the city of moss,
messengers that call the trees
down low

Small-strong, old
and tall black bones,
Old black bones
under that island

SERMONETTE

You're a young one, and should know
something of the way I had to go.
I learned to walk, then work, then pray.
To help without a thought of pay.

Made butter, syrup, soap and lard. Daydreamed
in the chicken yard.
And walked more than you will in years,
in tight, mail-order shoes from Sears.

Five miles we went, to school and back,
eatin' wild plums from a gunny sack.
Wasn't much school when the crops went in;
once harvest come, we went again.

That cotton! Kept our backs all bent;
Took a whole year's work to pay the rent.
Now, I did me a bit of lovin', too. Took the bitter and
the sweet when that come due.

Oh, but times were rich with food and light
at Christmas and on quiltin' night.

So the path gets hard! Don't mean it ain't good.
Now...that's just to be sure you understood.

ST. PAUL'S I

Built that church,
some of my people;
uncles an' cousins a' mine,
so I was always proud
to see Us
crossin' the green an' yellow
waves of earth
behind those ten black men
who walked from their fields
to this listenin' place.

Laid the lime,
Hauled the logs,
Cupped their hands
an' sealed the cracks.
Stamped their weight
into the foundation
an' christened the altar
with their sweat.

Saw a Black Self
stand up in their vision;
crowned
in the presence
of God.

ST. PAUL'S II

singin'
risin' as even
as sweetbread.

sometime
we get hold of a sound,
an' it just grow
an' grow, up to the middle of the roof;

altos an' tenors
float on up there
an' sit like homemade icing.

we'd cook that thing,
an' hush it down to cool!

then Soprano Sista Hazel
break in like rain,
sweep up the crumbs
an' wash it all down
from the wooden
bones of the Church, Yes, Lord!

We'd be baptized
in that music,
an' holdin'
hands
                    with spirits!

ST. PAUL'S III

seem like at Easter
the little church kinda
got its newness
Azalea an' honeysuckle chains
danced the crossin' beams
an' sweetened all our clothes

If we was poor
that day we didn't know it

you look back of your wagon
an' see the farmfolks
teeth whitened by the sun
heads up straight
an' their children
so clean an' combed
comin' like the colors of spring

BACK ROAD

sickness hangs on a nail
a yellow rag boiled too many times
to catch the life leaking out

I come back to the house
with my head low-down
for fear of seein' the men,
standin' together on the porch,
holdin' short answers to grief
in their folded arms
and the women
inside, movin' together
in twos and threes,
slow hands
ridin' dustcloud dresses

My momma went in the yellow
rag room
to watch Grandma dreamin';
Sissy went next, to see
what was keepin' her,
Auntie's out back now,
boilin' everything Grandpa touched;
ain't there a good word for this house?

I come back
with my head low-down
'cause I don't want them to see me
hatin' God while I cry

THREE

we was always together
when the work got done;
me an' E.B. an' Sammie Kate

three bites in the candy
from Mr. Frye's store
three wildflowers joinin' the fork road
at our meetin' place
with satin ribbons
trailin' the red-raw
hoops of dust

runnin' with our mouths
open so the sun fell in
and made us laugh
Loud an' Hard as we went

they was rich

'cause lemme tellya —
they was Rich Folks, honey;
keepin' two, three houses in different states,
makin' big phone calls outta town,
an' every time you turn around,
a party!
Crystal an' silver polish liked to rule my life!
An' nasty habits — Lord!
I seen 'em all, right there.
What?
Doin' for themselves?
Well, honey, they jus' didn't.

an' we?

we was treaters
an' placers
an' polishers;
eveners an'
stretchers an'
pullers;
dinnerwine pourers.
we was the cool black hand
under the brocade smile.
from the backstairs to the frontyard,
you'd find us, movin' these folks around
in they safeguarded lives.

Know that house so well, we could
stan' in the hall an'
hear money, just repeatin' itself,
multiplyin' an' addin' up; whisperin'
in the silk winda shades.

The place was perfumed with the greasy
smell of money—yes, it was—
but Rich Folks didn't like to pay ya none,
no-o-oo! Uh-Unh!
Give you a lace dress for the baby
an' a two dollar bill!

But we made it, honey, yes
an' some of us even did well.

MAKE WAY

rag of an apron
bitten stump of broom
milkweed and sunlight
streaming dead houses
tracks of all those
gone North

preachers with mended suitcases
millworkers and dayworkers
washwomen and drivermen

church-blessed and fates
fed to front porch
conversations

all those gone North
in narrow backs
and baggage cars of trains

with their trunks and shoulder wraps
with their traveling shoes
and careful dollar bills

LEAVIN'

I lit the stove that mornin'
   wearin' my Tuesday dress;
Lit the stove that mornin', early,
   wearin' my Tuesday dress;
Felt like a load of nothin';
   Had to try an' do my best.

Black wind through my dreamin',
   Sat me straight up in bed;
Black wind swept my dreamin', that night,
   Sat me straight up in bed
Walked the porch and wondered,
   Was it true what night wind said:

"Sunshine with no windows,
   Seven dollars' worth of sweat;
Sunshine with no windows, burnin',
   Seven dollars' worth of sweat.
On this land," said the night wind,
   "you always pays more than you get."

Took the kitchen road like always,
   Past the old shed made of tin;
Took the road to Cotter's kitchen, walkin',
   Past the old shed made of tin,
An' when I reached the doorway,
   A part of me would not go in.

Nothin' in old Cotter's
   after that day, looked the same;
Nothin' in that whole place, ever,
   after that day looked the same.
Gettin' outta Georgia,
   on a crowded, northboun' train.
Said I'm gettin' outta Georgia, leavin',
   on a crowded northboun' train.

30TH STREET STATION: NOVEMBER, 1943

I

This elastic woman
of the red dirt

This oak and elm daughter
of the plow

stepped down
from the howling belly
of the train

stared down
on stepfathers with iron tongues
landlords
and uniform smiles

climbed up
a polished pyramid of stairs
beside firm children
to look on Philadelphia;

to find her husband, shouting
in front of strangers,
his face
swimming wide
over winter

II

The smell of seasons
    ending/beginning deep in
        the tracks of her hands

SHORT LETTER: 1943

pray as I know you will,
Mom, we're catching Hell.
no night comes
when knives and bayonets
don't shine.
and here, lately,
a sour, grey stripe
in the morning breeze
tells me somebody's missing.

all the willing bones...blistered hands...
birthmarks...all the children
these men would have made
cross bloodlines
and fade under boots.

nobody really sleeps.
nobody knows the difference,
as we walk and crawl and stumble,
whispering to ourselves.

SOLOMON ISLANDS: 1945

we dug in our guns
on a lavender beach
last night

we counted the number
of lifetimes
to leap and fall
under the cabaret-bright
hills

Death swallowed the air
like a Biblical storm
churning the bowels
of the island,
eating the shadows
off our hands

The difference in night
and morning was
the holy stillness of
so many bodies without breath;

the doorway that somehow
we stumbled through,
so Death could suck
the sun from our black bones

UNDER FIRE

    Imagine sound:
coins,
soaked in glass,
slip from the mouth of
a dead man
as he speaks.

AFTER THE RAID

    Imagine
a mile of men,
hammered into blood-soaked sand,
sleeping like totems.

CHRISTMAS ON SAN FRANCISCO BAY: 1945

I

Home to slanted shores
Deep black blues play predictions
to soldiers on ships

II

Combing the multicolored
waters of the world
we come in many hundreds,
fragments of the great machine,
many hungers between our teeth,
smoking like grenades.

Reflections
soak the ships
and the water around them,
painting some men thick,
and others, not at all.

The Bay gives up no snipers,
no signals,
just the pulse of black lips,
gliding in sleep.

Just this new jungle
of Fords and Chryslers,
legs with no stockings on,
made with a likeness to mangoes,
music leaning out of windows.

WARRIOR CLASS: 1946

I am a nigger
that knows how to kill
a bringer of bloody fantasies

I am a wick
inside this uniform
waiting to be lit

every white punk
sails his noose,
laughing
in the path of my feet

every white punk knows
it's a good laugh
a belly rocker

shoulders
shakin' a bottle of
corn whiskey

every one of us
kicks it clear
or grinds the knot to thread

or stands still
like you do in the light
of a wild dog's eyes

SHORT STORY

A fine old gentleman closes the shop,
and its dull face dares the empty street.
Out back, the light smiles
through the eyes of the door
as men wait for its arm to open.

Black men in the black air,
waiting for cuts and shaves.

Loud boots from the sawmill
claim the floor
and flush the smell of
the sheriff's baggy flanks.

Then the old gent dances the broom;
Then they laugh til they lean way over.

Laugh,
and touch like brothers,
hunched. Backslapping hard together.
Yellow tears
ride down with laughter
in the fringe
of falling beards.

The shop is open now for closed men,
so tides of rage
can stagger the dead parts of them.

The line-standing blues.

The scarred remains of
colored regiments still at war.

The shop is open now
for closed men
so they can hold their fire
with mortar and spit,
mixed in the way
It Should Have Been.

Then they laugh
til they lean
way over.

AFTER THE RAID: 1943

I dreamed of kitchens
  and kitchen smells
    an Georgia Sea Island grass
      bandaged my sleep

One moon
    full of forgiveness
    resurrected my father's voice
      in a cylinder of light

Cutting through the sky,
 Cutting through the carnival of blood
    the sick results
      of men making peace,

Daddy's voice came
  sliding out,
    whole and recovered,
    whole and strong

      And gave the benediction
      before the day.

THE CLERK AT KELLEY'S GROCERY: 1938

white sails
deliver the names:
places like Quantico
and Mystic,
wind
up my blood rivers,
seeking a tongue,
a harbor.

loosed liquid
whispers
my redbone hands,
retreating
to its loud heart;
an ocean breaks
the world open.

seeping from shelves
of mustard, peanuts
and rice sacks,
a shoreline
teases my lips

Sailors
at the dock
Whistle me down—
Nothing but a bunch
of wet Northern boys
turned to tissue paper
by this Georgia heat.

"Here comes the boy!"
For all their
exuberant talk,
so glad to see me
Spinning chrome wheels
and cool cardboard—
"Here comes the boy!"

Sunday picnics
and weekend
caddy jobs
can't stop the sound

Summer-blooming
Baptist girls
in Sunday blouses
can't hush it.

MIGRANTS IN GERMANTOWN

whole families slept
down at the Center sometimes;
black farmers from
the hot-hurricane South,
plowed up by bad crops
and Klan.

Neighbors who knew
the homeground
shook their heads
across back fences
and felt it.

We folded blankets.
We followed,
squatting at steps and doorways
to watch the big folks move,
and pinch their sturdy love with smiles.

Down the cellar
for carrots and sage,
bringin' soup
to the Center again

starin' at the stares
of those country kids
broke something open
like Christmas

and set our feet
lightly
on a ripening road.

NIGHT SHIFT/DAY SHIFT

the trolleys click
like metronomes

measuring
the unconcealed prayers
of your mother
or mine; from the window
I smell their talcum
and see their houses,
calm and folded
buddhas on fat haunches,
curtains waving white
as bridal gloves.

bending, washing
standing and ironing
swings the breasts
like a rosary,
planting secret screams
deep in their
mysterious laps;
the soft sides of their arms
collecting steam and soap.

a wide-skirted
black dance
rustles cloth
in a cedar chest;
the reverent
feet of midwives
carry the sound.

a pendulum
of female motion
keeps the coin jar full.

DAY'S WORK

it was she who connected night
to the next day, daylight
to the night before, havin' walked
half-asleep from our place
to the kitchen

when the sun broke on that house
like neon in the daytime
it stood there,
square and clean and straight as good white teeth,
no corners unsure of their spindly legs;
no foundation
testing the next rain.
its broad back caught the sun
and threw the glass-gold crumbs to us

her sweat commanded the noon-high house
as she swept the big veranda,
trying to catch bony black sight of
her childrens' legs pecking the dirt lane.
cotton dresses in the chicken yard.

she picked his lemonade clean of imperfections,
scrubbed toilets and children,
kissed the iron many times with her moist finger
watching it turn hard clothes to butter.
ending the day
in the kitchen,
with carrots and apples in the folds
of her apron,
the sun fell behind her shoulders.

Standing in the cedar closet,
she heard herself
calling out for God
and the syrup-heavy sound of her children.

FIRST WINTER IN THE CITY

Snow,
coming like grey doves
landing in twos

Ella,
waiting for a bus
in the bakery door

Meanwhile,
passing over a place
that knew her name

Stirring
cold, tin-bucket mornings
with a long-handled spoon:

> *sewing*
> *on Saturday afternoons,*
> *burlap potato sacks,*
>
> *grinning bushels of fruit,*
> *and Daddy,*
> *who stopped all music with*
> *stricken eyes,*
> *who hushed us away*
> *while he remembered slavery.*

Past the screaming and singing
and reciting she knew
voices that would thicken and stay
past the iridescent hum, the flowers
past all the memory she was made of
Calling down her womanhood

Finally the wagon ride
to the train,
past the screaming and singing
and reciting she knew;
voices that would thicken and stay
past all the memory she was made of

Calling down her womanhood
churning thunder and corn and seedling days
down into the earth
Days that were done growing
in the white teeth of this city

No chickens trotting
by the legs of a girl
from the country

Bosses touching
Men staring
when they looked in her face

MEN, HONEY

Honey, most of these mens
wears travlin' shoes;
Gotta make 'em speak straight
so you don't get confused

If he's talkin' fast
and you're talkin' slow,
Better realize you got
a longer ways to go

If you're at prayer meetin'
and he's at the Game,
Gotta know, Girl—
your heads ain't turned the same

Oh, but get yourself one
of those half-good types,
that's pretty but lazy
and got the gripes—

Don't force love on 'im
if he wants to be free;
You'll end up with a baby
too big for your knee!

Now if you run up
on one that's good,
don't treat him too much
like Mama would

You stay bent over
to prop him up,
you're gonna get drained
like a drinkin' cup,

But if you rise like the sun
and shine like brass,
you'll get plenty 'tention
and won't have to ask!

AFTER PRAYER MEETIN'

many was the time
I missed my stop,
laughin' on the bus with Benjamin
we were sweethearts
on the old PTC line;
That man could
get me laughin'
til the breeze
wrapped around my legs!

Not a fancy man, that Ben,
but Lord, he loved ice cream!
Harbison's vanilla
in pink crystal bowls
for Wednesdays
after prayer meetin'

The mind only holds so much
an' even that comes and goes,
but some things I remember
rich and regular:
    his reliable hands,
    protecting my waist like a new stem;
    his coffee-with-no-cream skin;
    lemon soap
    an' cotton creases under my iron.

We stood some good earth together...

AN OLD HOUSE

It's an old story,
this house,
'bout as old as me,
and we only got
a few wrinkled pages
left to read.

Yes, we done got old together.

When the teenagers go by
with that dern music boilin',
I say a prayer for my house
and my head—
                What they gonna know about
                makin' 18 dollars a week
                and needin' a quiet place in this world?
                ...I could tell 'em
Winter was the Thing
that brought me here,
with a wind that had my teeth rattlin'
like beans in a dry pot!

Didn't buy a living thing
for two years straight
to save that money;
Didn't hardly have spit
to lick a stamp!
'Cause I promised the Lord
I'd do better...

It's an old comfort-spot now,
an' I'm as warm as I wanna be, sittin' here—
watchin' my crystal turn
the color of sunlight

JOHNNY TATE REMEMBERS: 1952

bald eyes
buldging youth

Free, come Friday,
of slamdowns
at the factory
drunk Irish spit
at the gate

The Four Horsemen slide
every Saturday night,
spiking hearts
on starch-white collar tips

Mighty eagle
flies green delirium
on the avenue

Short glasses toting
heavy liquids
Peacock lashes
obeying blue-green lids

Buick bebopping,
the Four go high
looping rides
over the bandstand
down the slopes
into the valley
of breasts

GEORGIA
to my grandmother Georgia Hook McMichael

your sister speaks of you
but it is slow,
traveling down the history
of braids around her grey head
to the smell of Carolina
and your wide waist
standing at a country blackboard

I might have visited,
and laid in a high bed,
riding toward sleep
on the geechee strings
of half-white aunts
and cousins who are strange to me
gathered bark for sassafras,
or tried to snap the beans
the way you did

Grandma, I have been away so long
and you, much longer;

Claiming you now,
the one left
with your melon face
and the sloping road
hung in your eyes,
walking south.

GREEN COTTON

she laughed
louder than us
rode our bikes
made us dolls

We smelled
her clothes
called her hard hair "country,"
giggled at her breasts

> *You were the gift*
> *who came crouching*
> *Hit by a man*
> *who made you run*

> *Eveline the oldest*
> *last to come,*
> *Born in the doorway*
> *Born in the middle of the night*

How the sun came up
in her face and kissed it
when she talked about
'Down home'

How her skin
was shiny dark
as new chestnuts,
hidden in those sharp pods

> *I was the first*
> *to find you*
> *sleeping in a summer dress*
> *green with parrots*

> *No coat*
> *and no Mama*
> *A Tennessee-ripe girl*
> *standing by the stove*

She took us through walls
at night
riding stories
in high grass

Naming the whole
wide meadow
from
the swayback of a mile

HILL SCHOOL

me and Julietta and Jean
with flowers
around our ears,
twisting and twitching and
about to bust,
waiting to dance
the dance of the fairies,
and for once
be sure of our beauty.

oh, you should've seen it!
the neighborhood turned out
when May Day came.
pink paper streamers
and grandparents in folding chairs
filled the schoolyard, right up to
our stage...

and somewhere,
at the edge of the crowd
was Papa (who rehearsed our recitations),
sharp as a tack
in his weary suit.
His crescent smile
ready with all
the missing words.

FOREMOTHERS
to my grandmother Anna Mae Ellison Chaney

Chocolate-pitted fruit on a dying vine
Raisin-faced women with African eyes,
Making city madness into southern shine

Wrinkled flower petals singing wrinkled rhyme
Bodies bent over brooms, sweeping dusty lies;
Chocolate-pitted fruit on a dying vine

Hanging up daydreams on somebody's line
In their hardwork-hands the womanness dries,
Making city madness into southern shine

They fatten the children at visiting time
Carrying bakery bags as their prize,
Chocolate-pitted fruit on a dying vine

On whispering memory they recline
Recalling cow's milk, the first-born cries;
Making city madness into southern shine

The grassy back-door lane, the Georgia pine
Their lessons leave us wisdom in disguise,
Chocolate-pitted fruit on a dying vine
Making city madness into southern shine

PROPHESY

she was going to stride
like stone, They said, into slack jaws
going to sprinkle fever
on the flock,
that long-legged one.
going to tremble the Sunday word
into each day. They saw
the call in her orderly face.
Miss Gert, born with a veil of knowingness,
said it too: "That girl's gonna preach!"

while she laughed at her feet
making wine
on the Italian porch
of her neighbors,
while she pressed her voice
like a woman
through the curtains
of the rectangle house,
They added reason to her ways.

On the corner, crossed arms conferred.
In the kitchens They knew it;
Not even noddin' their heads.

ABOUT PRESENCE

old voices crackle
on stern grave stoves,
attest to vital threads and leaves,
cricket songs on silent paths,
guts, boiled hard to commit
memory.

old voices caress
the humming woods,
the morning mist,
the unseen sakes
and souls.